RAW

FRANCES BRIGGS

PHOTOGRAPHY BY

FRANCES JANISCH,
PETER BAASCH &
DARON CHATZ

Struik Publishers (Pty) Ltd
80 McKenzie Street
Cape Town
8001
South Africa
Reg. no.: 54/00695/07
First published in 2000
10 9 8 7 6 5 4 3 2

ISBN 1 86872 510 3

Designer: Petal Palmer
Publishing manager: Linda de Villiers
Editor: Gail Jennings
Proofreader: Brenda Brickman
Reproduction by Hirt & Carter Cape (Pty) Ltd
Printed and bound by Craft Print (Pte) Ltd, Singapore

PHOTOGRAPHIC CREDITS

A = Architect © = Copyright L = Location

Listed in order: Photographer, Stylist and Architect/Copyright holder/Location
Photographers: FJ = Frances Janisch, DC = Daron Chatz FB = Frances Briggs, PB = Peter Baasch, CF = Craig Fraser
Architects: JS = Johann Slee, SR = Sylvio Rech, PL = Pierre Lombart, KO = Kate Otten, CG = Charl Groenewald
Stylists: FB = Frances Briggs, LJ = Laura Jamieson COC = Cathy O'Cleary, LF = Lynn Fraser NVW = Natalie van Wyk, KN = Kassie Naidoo
Locations: LOTB = The Lodge on the Bay, SAP = St Augustine's Priory, T = Timbuktu
Copyright holders ELLE Decoration = *Elle Decoration* Magazine, ELLE = *Elle Magazine*, SLV = St Leger & Viney

Cover, from left: FJ/FB/JS(A); FJ/COC/ELLE Decoration©; DC/FB/PL(A); PB/ELLE©; page 2: FJ/FB/JS(A); page 6, clockwise from top left: DC/LJ/LOTB(L); DC/FB/PL(A); PB/FB/SR(A); FJ/COC/ELLE Decoration©; FJ/SAP(L); DC/LJ/LOTB(L); DC/LJ/LOTB(L); FJ/LJ/ELLE Decoration©; PB/COC/ELLE Decoration©; page 10: DC/FB/PL(A); page 13: DC/FB/PL(A); page 14: DC/FB/PL(A); page 15 left and right: DC/FB/PL(A); pages 16-7: FJ/FB/JS(A); page 18: DC/FB/PL(A); page 19: DC/LJ/ELLE Decoration©; page 20: DC/LJ/ELLE Decoration©; page 21: PB/COC/ELLE Decoration©; page 22: FJ/SAP(L); page 22: CF/ELLE Decoration©; page 24 left: PB/FB/SR(A); page 24 right: DC/FB; page 25: FJ/KO(A); page 26: FJ/SAP(L); page 27: FJ/SAP(L); Page 28: DC/FB/PL(A); page 31: FJ/LJ/ELLE Decoration©; page 32: PB/COC/ELLE Decoration©; page 33: PB/COC/ELLE Decoration©; page 34: DC/FB/PL(A); page 35: DC/FB/PL(A); page 36 left and right: PB/COC/ELLE Decoration©; page 37 right: FB (stylist and photographer); pages 38-9: DC/FB/JS(A); page 40: DC/LJ/LOTB(L); page 41, clockwise from top left: FJ/FB; DC/FB; FJ/FB; page 42: FJ/FB/JS(A); page 43: DC/LJ/ELLE Decoration©; page 44 left and right: DC/FB/PL(A); page 45: DC/FB/PL(A); pages 46-7: DC/FB/JS(A); page 48, clockwise from top left: FB (stylist and photographer); FB (stylist and photographer); FJ; DC/FB; DC/LOTB(L); DC; DC; PB; DC/LJ/ELLE Decoration©; page 50: FJ/FB/JS(A); page 53: PB/COC/ELLE Decoration©; page 54 left: PB/COC/ELLE DECORATION©; page 54 right: DB/COC/ELLE DECORATION©; page 55: FJ/COC/ELLE Decoration©; pages 56-7: FJ/FB/JS(A); page 58: FJ/COC/ELLE Decoration©; page 59: PB/COC/KO(A); page 60-1: FJ/COC/ELLE Decoration©; page 61 right: FJ/COC/ELLE Decoration©; page 62 FJ/FB/JS(A); page 63 PB/COC/ELLE Decoration©/KO(A); page 64 top and below: DC/COC/CG(A); page 65: DC/COC/CG(A); page 66: FJ/COC/ELLE Decoration©; page 67 top: PB/COC/ELLE Decoration©; page 67 below: DC/FB/JS(A); page 68: PB/FB/SR(A); page 69: DC/COC/CG(A); page 70: DC/ELLE Decoration©; page 73: PB/COC/ELLE Decoration©; page 74-5: DC/FB/PL(A); page 75: PB/COC/ELLE Decoration©; page 76 clockwise from top left: PB/COC/ELLE Decoration©; DC/LJ/LOTB(L); FJ/FB; PB/COC/ELLE Decoration©; page 77: DC/LJ/LOTB(L); page 78: FJ/LJ/ELLE Decoration©; page 79 top: FJ/LJ/ELLE Decoration©; page 79 below: FB (photographer); page 80 left: DC/LJ/ELLE Decoration©; page 80 right: DC/LJ/LOTB(L); page 81 left: DC/LJ/LOTB(L); page 81 right: DC/LJ/ELLE DECORATION©; page 82: FJ/COC/ELLE Decoration©; page 85: PB/COC/ELLE DECORATION©; page 86 left: PB/COC/ELLE Decoration©; page 86 right: DC/LJ/ELLE Decoration©; page 87: FJ/COC/ELLE DECORATION©; page 87 right: PB/KN/ELLE©; pages 88-89: FJ/ELLE Decoration©; page 90: PB/FB/SR(A); page 91: PB/COC/ELLE Decoration©; page 92: PB/KN/ELLE©; page 93: PB/COC/ELLE Decoration©; page 94: PB/FB/SR(A); page 95: FJ/FB/JS(A); page 96 top and below: FJ/FB; page 97: PB/FB/SR(A); pages 98-99: FJ; page 100: DC/FB; page 101: DC/FB; page 102: PB/ELLE©; page 105: PB/COC/T(L); page 106: DC/COC/SLV©; page 107 top, centre and below: DC/COC/SLV©; page 108 left and right: DC/COC/SLV©; page 109: DC/COC/SLV©; pages 110-11: FJ/COC/ELLE Decoration©; page 110 right: PB/COC/ELLE Decoration©; page 112 clockwise from top left: DC/LJ/LOTB(L); DC/COC/ELLE Decoration©; DC/COC/ELLE Decoration©; DC/LJ/ELLE Decoration©; PB/COC/ELLE Decoration©; DC/LJ/LOTB(L); DC/LJ/LOTB(L); pages 114-15: PB/LJ/ELLE Decoration©; page 116: DC/LJ/ELLE Decoration©; DC/LJ/LOTB(L); page 118: FJ/FB; page 119: FJ/FB/JS(A); Page 120: FJ/COC/ELLE Decoration©; page 121 top: PB/COC/ELLE©; page 121 below: PB/NVW/ELLE Decoration©; page 122: FJ/COC/ELLE Decoration©; page 125: DC/LF/ELLE Decoration©; page 126 left: FJ/COC/ELLE Decoration©; page 126 right PB/COC/ELLE Decoration©; page 127 left and right: PB/COC/ELLE©; page 128: DC/LJ/LOTB(L); page 129: DC/LJ/ELLE Decoration©; page 130: DC/LJ/ELLE Decoration©; page 131: PB/LJ/ELLE Decoration©; page 132: DC/LJ/ELLE Decoration©; page 133: DC/FB/JS(A); page 134, clockwise from top left: PB/COC/ELLE Decoration©; DC/LJ/ELLE Decoration©; PB/LJ/ELLE Decoration©; DC/LJ/ELLE Decoration©; PB/COC/ELLE Decoration©; DC/LJ/ELLE Decoration©; DC/FB; PB/COC/ELLE Decoration©; DC/LJ/ELLE Decoration©; page 136 top and below: FB (stylist and photographer; page 137: FJ/FB; page 138: DC/LJ/ELLE ELLE Decoration©; page 139: DC/LJ/ELLE Decoration©; page 140 top and below right: FJ/COC/ELLE Decoration©; page 140 below left: DC/LJ/ELLE Decoration©; page 141: FJ/COC/ELLE Decoration©

AUTHOR'S ACKNOWLEDGEMENTS

Heartfelt thanks to Uschi and Peter Stuart, Rita and Chris Blignaut, Mavis Briggs, Leana Swanepoel, Frances, Daron, Peter, Cathy, all the architects and the team at Struik for their generous help in making this book happen.

RAW

RAW

RAW

INTRODUCTION

In a world that is increasingly demanding, there is no better 'rescue remedy' than to connect with nature. Feeling the earth beneath our bare feet or lying on a patch of grass and staring at the clouds overhead is pure bliss. These simple pleasures keep us in touch with the rhythms of our natural environment. And on a deep level, they nurture and nourish our souls.

Before the rapid urbanisation of the past few centuries, people would build their homes using raw materials gleaned from the earth and vegetation around them. They lived close to the natural world and used natural materials, imbued with 'good vibrations'.

Today it is these vibrations we yearn for, to ground us and offer a calm centre within the whirlwind.

Unfortunately much of this building knowledge has been lost to us. We no longer sleep and live in circular structures close to the ground as our ancestors did. Our homes are raised above the ground or separated by concrete foundations, with no connection to the earth. We are surrounded by artificial light and plastic surfaces. It is this separation from nature that leaves us feeling scattered and burnt out.

Today, many of us try to make sanctuaries out of our living spaces. Here we attempt to escape from the encroaching complexity of modern life, with its electromagnetically charged computers and mobile phones.

Never before has there been a time when the pull of nature has been stronger – not just for a weekend away in the country, but in our everyday lives.

Our approach to creating living spaces should be holistic, functional and sensual, but most of all, reflect the essence of who we are. One of the ways in which we can do this is by surrounding ourselves with a 'living' environment, one that takes its inspiration from the natural world. We are real people who need to live in real spaces – we are not creators of spaces for others to admire for a season or so until the next fad comes along.

Living space is sacred. It is our inner kingdom. It is a place to enjoy good food, friendship and fun – a refuge for relaxation, contemplation and rejuvenation, where privacy and comfort are essential.

You don't have to spend a fortune to create an environment that inspires you and tantalises your senses. Great beauty may be found in small things. Enjoy the transitory gifts of each season by collecting treasures such as twigs, pebbles and wild grasses, and extend that simple beauty to your home. Arrange your other personal treasures to reflect your mood.

The renewal of each season allows us to renew ourselves. Breathe new life into areas that have cocooned you through the stillness of winter, or prepare for the new life of spring with a good cleansing. Reinvent a room in a day by changing fabrics or finding new homes for old paintings. Experiment with changing the position of your bed to alter your perspective completely.

The possibilities are endless, the palette dizzying, and the potential unlimited.

Raw need not be rustic, unfinished or untreated. It's about layering the old with the new. Think shiny with smooth, or rough and textured. The focus is on mixing the natural with modern convenience. Raw materials are timeless, suited to all styles of decorating, and by their nature they belong in any environment.

In this book you'll find both relaxed and sophisticated ways to incorporate raw materials into building and design. With down-to-earth simplicity it's easy to create a living-friendly atmosphere – one that's timeless, functional, stylish and affordable.

RAW

RAW
METAL

Metals do not simply serve a practical purpose. They offer reflective surfaces that may be beaten, oxidised or left in a silvery smooth pristine state to create architectural designs and artistic expressions. Whatever effect you wish to achieve, metal has a place in decoration.

Modern designs include metal for functionality. Iron and steel fortify structures as well as beautify them. Wrought iron, galvanised metal, stainless steel, pewter and aluminium all enhance architectural designs. Corrugated iron is affordable and practical as a roofing material most suited to South Africa's climate — particularly if one enjoys the sound of rain hitting the roof during a thunderstorm.

Stainless-steel surfaces are practical in modern kitchens — and look spectacular when fashioned onto the façades of buildings — where they offer a cool contrast to warmer materials. Wrought iron is crafted for solid railings, staircases or garden accessories and outdoor furniture. In recent years aluminium and pewter have been shaped into decorative cutlery, door handles, napkin rings and frames. Increasingly important for structural purposes too, aluminium and steel add reflective edginess to contrast with subtle and soothing opposites.

Innovative and trendy artisans now recycle scrap metals to sculpture functional artworks, expressing another side to the often mundane uses of metal. In its various forms and reflective values, metal has found an integral place in decoration and design. Always cool to the touch, metal delivers a refreshing and soothing effect on all interiors.

PREVIOUS PAGE: Industrial metal sheeting has been custom cranked to a specific radius, creating the effect of a domed ceiling. The walls have been kept white to emphasise clean architectural lines.
RIGHT: Reflective utilitarian surfaces made of cool, blue stainless steel deliver a refreshingly functional yet stylish edge to this understated modern kitchen.

LEFT AND BELOW: This metal staircase, which connects two floors, was created by two South African artists, Guy du Toit and David Rossouw. A functioning, living piece of art, it is sculpted from construction metal. Each step embodies the different elements – earth, air, fire, metal and water – using different materials. The staircase also

features a fan, pieces of broken glass and running water. From every angle in this house there is visual interaction with the symmetry of wood and metal.

RIGHT: In this open-plan kitchen, the

silvery metallic curves of the stainless-

steel door handles and industrial light

fittings combine well with the earthy

colours of the plastered walls and

limestone floors.

LEFT: Get away from it all without leaving home in

this bedroom designed with a flushed metal ceiling.

Pale colours, wooden floors and minimal decorating

are the ingredients of this serene, uncluttered space.

From the window you can gaze across a vast horizon and enjoy majestic sunsets.

ABOVE: A metal rail and acacia cotton hanging shelf have been used to create this simple

and practical storage solution, which allows clothing to breathe.

PREVIOUS PAGES: In the loving hands of a master crafter,

metal may be beaten and bent

into whimsical shapes. Naively

plastered walls have been

spontaneously dotted with

coloured glass and confidently

coated in vibrant hues.

ABOVE: Scour street markets for home accessories such as

this bent-wire bath rack.

RIGHT: A family kitchen with 'industrial-strength' style.

ABOVE: Custom-designed wrought-iron railings and animal-design patio

furniture add a whimsical flavour to outdoor spaces.

RIGHT: On the exterior of this modern home, corrugated metal has been

sculpted into the integral design. Plastered walls and paving celebrate the

use of raw material and create an impressive façade.

LEFT AND RIGHT:

Metal may seem an

unusual element to use

in an interior, because of

its hard, steely and often

cold appearance. Yet in most forms – as seen here with this simple

painted kitchen table with a metal top – it adds a cool contrast to warmer

raw materials. In recent years, metals such as aluminium, pewter and

stainless steel have become popular materials for everyday items that

are functional yet artistic.

RAW

RAW

WOOD

The numbing melange of endless traffic jams and grey buildings makes most people yearn for quiet and a sense of order. We look to the trees in lush indigenous forests and fragrant pine plantations for their magnificent healing nature. We use the expression 'touch wood', which seems to imbue wood with sacred powers and protective qualities.

Wood has been used for centuries for construction, work surfaces and art forms. Wood appeals to our senses; we intuitively touch those surfaces that capture our attention. Unusual knotty grains and textures delight the eye, while subtle aromas linger long after the tree has left the forest.

Wood shares a sympathetic symbiosis with nature by aesthetically fusing with all other raw materials.

Think eco-friendly before buying timber. Ensure that the wood comes from sustainable sources, where it is quickly replenished. Better suppliers will have a good forestry policy and should know the properties and qualities of each wood. Whenever possible, recycle old wood.

Forests function as the lungs of the earth; they purify and cleanse the air we breathe, and add grace to our landscapes. It is essential that each of us plays our part in preserving this precious resource.

PREVIOUS PAGE: Nothing could be simpler than using scaffolding planks from bluegum trees for wooden flooring, such as these found in a builders' yard. The design of this house allows the wood to be visible from all angles. With more people working from home these days, living spaces are being redefined by their flexibility to evolve into work spaces.
RIGHT: A single aluminium lamp offers stark contrast to an organic palette of ochre-pigmented, roughly plastered walls and ageing wood. Cool concrete slabs for shelving and sleek modern surfaces tempered with earthy and weathered textures, create a crucial balance.

PREVIOUS PAGES: In this idyllic

country cabin, the walls, ceiling, floor

and even tables and chairs are made

from different varieties of wood. The

sleek lines of contemporary furniture

and Zen-inspired jug and bowls offer streamlined simplicity against a rustic backdrop.

LEFT: The levels seem to soar to lofty heights in this home; the environment seems to expand

endlessly. The myriad patterns, shapes and textures of wood found here can be combined with

other raw materials, in ways to suit tastes that are organic or urban chic.

ABOVE: Integration of outdoor and indoor makes this generous space seem even more generous.

The symmetry of wood and its knotty appearance adds textural interest. Wind-block windows and

large door openings have been designed to allow in cool breezes and an abundance of natural light.

ABOVE AND RIGHT: If it is protected, wood weathers well against natural

forces. However, over-exposure to sun, wind and rain will wear wooden doors

and window frames over time, eventually resulting in an appealing bleached

look with characteristic cracks. To nourish and preserve raw wood, regularly

apply coats of thinned linseed oil or beeswax with a soft rag.

RIGHT: In this fusion of East and West and old and new, a contemporary dining suite composed of artificial and natural materials coexists with a lustrous wooden floor and the intricate hand-carvings on the display cabinet from India. The floor has a painted trompe l'oeil carpet, appropriately breaking up a large, neutral space with a colourful, artistic alternative.

LEFT AND THIS PAGE: As we bring the elements of texture, light, form and colour into our own environment by using raw materials, we strengthen our connection to the earth. Here, a naive arrangement of twigs and branches in a glass, with carved wooden cups and bowls from North Africa and Indonesia, have been placed to reflect the mood of the moment.

LEFT: Polished teak beams with bluegum poles spaced intermittently between them add an informal

touch to the muted family room. Two wooden armoires balanced proportionately in the room are

complemented by knotty kelims, which cover a concrete floor, and Art Deco chairs.

ABOVE: A comforting space with the bare essentials: a burning candle, second-hand wooden table

with home-made shelf and fairytale wrought-iron furniture.

RIGHT: Chairs made from laminated plywood are left in their original state, unmoulded

and uncovered. They have been fitted with metal castors, allowing the chairs to move and

swivel freely. Inspirational in design yet functional for entertaining, this dining room may

also be transformed into an informal boardroom for impromptu meetings.

BELOW: This open-plan space is joined by a seamless, suspended catwalk, which

separates the guest suite from the main bedroom and bathroom in this home.

Internal windows and skylights allow light to flood the inner sanctum.

PREVIOUS PAGES: In this urban family kitchen, naturally scented cedar-wood cabinets have been limewashed for a bleached, matte look that contrasts with the polished granite surfaces and the sleek metal stove unit. Easy-to-clean concrete floors, tinted to organic hues with powdered pigments, have been scored into symmetrical slabs and sealed with linseed oil.

LEFT: Wood appeals to all our senses. Its availability, plus the ease with which it can be transformed and shaped, has made it an ideal material for buildings objects and creating sculptural carvings.

Indulge in collecting wooden items. Whether traditionally made modern pieces or timeless treasures, structural beams or objets d'art, wood reflects a character and warmth that synthetic materials simply do not have.

RAW

RAW
PLASTER

Whether mixed with water and smeared onto a floor, petrified over time into stone or baked into bricks, earth has been the most common material since the beginning of time.

Where regions lack timber and stone, indigenous peoples use earth itself to build their homes. Many may simply daub the framework of a hut with mud. Modern humans have refined this method with synthetic materials such as cement, concrete and plaster, all suited to harsh climates and the demanding modern lifestyle. Adobe, raw plaster and clay have natural insulation properties and the added pleasure of the delicate, sweet aroma of earth.

Homes made from earth-coloured plaster, brick or clay are the epitome of living in the raw. These houses usually feel cool and blend in with the natural environment. The style can be continued indoors with minimal decoration and natural fabrics and fibres. Highly durable and able to withstand normal traffic, plastered walls and floors are naturally handsome.

Plastered walls can have a deep, textural relief or a smooth, sophisticated hardness, depending on application. In most cases plaster can be tinted to a variety of shades, using powdered pigments and oxides. Plastering techniques can imitate the cool effect of stone or chalky frescoed walls, revolutionising wall coverings and the feeling of space.

PREVIOUS PAGE: Plaster may be tinted to a variety of subtle, earthy shades using coloured pigments and powdered oxides.
RIGHT: This creamy wall has been trowelled to a smooth finish for a sophisticated look. The plaster was then sealed with tinted wax.

BELOW AND RIGHT: Plastered walls offer a refreshing retreat from the scorching summer sun. A friendly material to live with, raw plaster 'breathes' well, allowing moisture to evaporate easily. Walls textured with plaster are best left in their chalky, natural state or washed with the slightest tint of colour. Plastered walls combined with wooden floors work well for both urban chic and modern country styles.

PREVIOUS PAGES: Raw materials, as used on the exterior of this house, blend with the surrounding natural environment.

BELOW AND RIGHT: Textured, natural plaster walls have a different allure to that of the flat, synthetic surfaces of wallpaper, vinyl and paint. It is possible to texture plaster by scoring the

wet surface with an assortment of tools. Try adding coarse sea sand to the plaster mix for a slightly rougher finish. Or you could incise a border of small stones, river pebbles or crystals sunken in wet plaster.

In this photographic studio, hand-plastered walls combine well with a concrete floor to create a cool, earthy work space. Decorative metal work adds the personal, transforming finishing touches.

LEFT AND BELOW: In this kitchen, finely plastered walls have been smoothed to perfection and tinted an ochre hue. The concrete screed floor has been scored into large shapes to look like paving stones.

With its dark walnut unit and cool metal stove, the kitchen is fuss-free, functional, modern and elegant.

LEFT AND ABOVE: When wet, plaster can be manipulated and

transformed into any design. The amount of texture depends entirely

on the look you desire. Raw plaster has a warm and ancient

quality – the look is influenced by our African heritage.

Heavily textured plaster has an undiluted rustic appeal, which

can be tempered with sparse aluminium accessories.

LEFT AND RIGHT: Concrete is the modern equivalent of stone. In many aspects of contemporary architecture, it has taken the place of stone by offering a sense of weight and solidity with very little effort and cost. Left raw it has a distinctly industrial look, although its starkness can be softened with tints or paints, or in clever combination with timber and colourful fabrics.

The industrial effect of the concrete slabs punctuating the walls of this architect's home is warmed by Zimbabwean teak floors.

LEFT AND RIGHT: Concrete is truly the defining material of modern architecture, because of its afford-ability and minimalistic appearance.

It has given new meaning to the concept 'functionality'. Indoors it is most commonly found on floors, although it is also suited to shelving, built-in bed bases, benches, baths and other furniture. In this home, chunks of scored concrete slabs have been used to create the look of flagstones.

FOLLOWING PAGES: Textural qualities can be incorporated into any good architectural design, and are partic-ularly effective when making use of the available light.

RAW

MASONRY

Stone may be introduced in the home in the smallest of ways: an arrangement of stones around the base of a tree, in a jar or as a border of river pebbles embedded in the ground. On the other hand, you may decide on a solid stone house. Whichever style you choose, stone offers a way to celebrate the ordinary things from our amazingly abundant world.

Stone and brick may be married harmoniously with elements such as wood and metal; they support each other in an aesthetic and structural way.

The ancient media of brick and stone have always suggested antiquity and solidity. Each piece of stone is unique in shape and almost indestructible – it invariably improves with the weathering of time.

Sandstone, limestone, slate and other stones lend themselves to both structural building work and intricate or simple paving designs – mixed with standard building bricks or quarried tiles, stone will create a stunning visual patchwork with permanence.

PREVIOUS PAGE: An old wall has been stripped to its original state, revealing solid stone.
RIGHT: In this bathroom the mix of modern white tiles and rugged grey slate is easy to maintain.

LEFT: Building bricks have been used to create the floor in this modern architect's home. An industrial grinding machine was used to smooth and level the top surface.

ABOVE: This outdoor table top is made from a thick slab of grey slate.

LEFT: Use 'masonry' materials for simple decoration –

display beach pebbles and shells in bowls or baskets.

RIGHT: In this bathroom, a sensual palette of neutral

shades, sandstone tiles and beech flooring work in perfect

synergy. In the typical African heat, these materials offer

cool refreshment to tired and aching skin.

LEFT: This sleek, pale, maple side unit softens the effect of rough stone walls.

ABOVE AND RIGHT: Bricks are the basic building block of architectural evolution and the most common material used since the beginning of time. Used in minimal quantities, bricks add character to a room and have a warming influence; too much, however, tends to make spaces feel dark and imposing.

BELOW: This bathroom was created to provide the

ultimate sensual retreat. Pale and mottled glass mosaic

tiles lend purity to the shower, in sharp contrast to the

slate, which is rugged with dark, variegated colouring.

BELOW: Slate is remarkably versatile: it can function as interior or exterior flooring, or as paving, roofing or shelving material. It is available in many colours, from gold to blue, grey, charcoal and black. Slate co-ordinates with any decorating scheme, such as in this minimalist bathroom, where personal accessories like candles and incense suggest quiet contemplation and rejuvenation.

RAW

RAW
CERAMIC

Smooth and glazed or crude and rugged, ceramic materials imbue a rustic quality to surfaces and functional items. Natural, uncoloured clay tiles and pots are available in many sizes and colour variations, from deep, burnished browns to tawny reds and fiery golds, which add warmth to living spaces. The colours are usually influenced by the region in which the clay was found. Colour may also be affected by oils rising to the surface during firing, which create an authentic patina. An occasional injection of passionately coloured mosaic tiles creates a strong visual contrast to this organic palette.

Ceramists understand the behaviour of the materials they use, and know the best clay for each individual piece, whether it is a sculptural piece of art or a functional floor tile.

Ceramic materials are timeless, suited to all styles of decorating – try placing large clay bowls of cinnamon sticks on a festive table, or simply add a row of naively painted tiles for decoration. By its very nature, clay has a sense of belonging to the environment. In surrounding ourselves with earthen materials we are putting ourselves back in touch with the environment.

PREVIOUS PAGE: Yin and Yang ceramic bowls with chopsticks have been placed in minimal arrangement to create an informal dining setting. Simple and uncluttered, a stem of bamboo leaves stands in a wooden vase, offering a soothing splash of green.
RIGHT: Dipping bowls and plates in varying shades of celadon and sage green are multi-functional accessories that are also rewarding to the eye.

BELOW: Ceramics instantly add a sense of earthen goodness to an interior. Shapely platters and nomadic stoneware bowls make beautiful everyday items. They are at their best left in plain, earthy colours with a matte finish.

BELOW: An arrangement of stoneware bowls in various heights, sizes and styles creates a stunning and eclectic feature of curved forms and pristine lines. Ceramics may be finely glazed or burnished, or left naive, granular and rustic.

PREVIOUS PAGES: A ceramist's studio in the

Karoo overflows with works in progress.

LEFT AND ABOVE: The magnificent art of mosaic

has been practised for centuries. Small pieces of ceramic, stone or glass tesserae are placed

close together, embedded in wet cement in three-dimensional, whimsical designs. Mosaics can

be incorporated into any architectural design and made an integral part of the building.

BELOW AND RIGHT: Used to decorate table tops and shower floors or to surround a window or mirror frame, mosaics add a colourful artistic detail in geometric patterns or renditions of everyday scenes. They also enliven otherwise cold, stark surfaces.

This concrete screed floor and basin unit (RIGHT) are tinted blue and green to complement the bright mosaic tiles in the

shower, creating a pleasing visual symmetry. Roughly plastered walls add to the overall textural appeal. Mosaics look so simple, and it is certainly worth trying to create one yourself, but it does require patience and hard work. The design is fundamental and correct materials are essential. Begin with an old garden pot before trying out that floor you have in mind.

LEFT AND RIGHT:

Naive designs add a personal touch when decorating with mosaic.

A hand-painted ceramic

basin found in Mexico incorporates almost every colour under the sun. It is set

in concrete screed, which has been painted red. Copper laboratory piping and

taps are an innovative alternative to the standard items.

THIS PAGE AND RIGHT: Terracotta pots of all shapes and sizes, filled to the brim with flowers, culinary herbs or cactuses, make a simple, innovative sculptural feature when embedded into concrete or plastered walls. They offer an excellent solution for expansive stretches of exterior walls, or when growing miniature gardens. Ceramic pots and tiles may have natural colour variations on the surface, unique to every single piece; this is largely influenced by the region in which the clay is found.

PREVIOUS PAGES: This garden mosaic was created using loose pieces of marble left over from a cutting yard. Recycle marble, stone or glass to make your own designs at home.

LEFT AND RIGHT: Small, evenly shaped, glazed green tesserae combined with a matte stone inlay are set in a refined geometric border to magnificent effect on this wrought-iron table. Weatherproof and easy to clean, a mosaic table top is the practical choice for family breakfasts outside. At last mosaics are no longer used just for decorating swimming pools. Experiment with creating homemade mosaics incorporating shells, pebbles and crystals.

RAW

RAW

TEXTILES

Textiles are often the starting point to planning a decorating scheme. We may see a fabric with enormous appeal and begin to seek ways of using it. A vibrantly coloured kelim can be thrown over a sofa, or a simple sheet of muslin can be loosely draped over a open window.

Textiles are not only a way of adding colour to our interiors. They also introduce the element of texture, with their contrasting weaving techniques and innovative designs. These woven delights come in different thicknesses, textures and styles. They add warmth and comfort to tiles, floorboards or couches, and silky softness to bed linen.

For understated simplicity, dress cold areas with raw materials such as hemp or jute. On balmy days, keep fabrics sheer around windows to allow fresh breezes to diffuse through finely woven yarns.

For centuries, different cultures have woven mystical and magical legends into their textiles. Traditionally, people conveyed messages about their heritage, their family, their region or their religious faith, all through the patterns and colours they chose as they wove. In some cultures, woven textiles have great value and may represent a family's wealth.

Different patterns and textures lend themselves to different seasons throughout the year. In summer, stick to cool cotton. Keep the silk, cashmere and velvet for cooler weather.

PREVIOUS PAGE: Textured white waffle-weave cotton gown, socks and a blanket-stitched throw are inviting in cooler weather.
RIGHT: Vibrant cloths from North Africa are displayed here to their best advantage against a stone wall, which acts as a neutral backdrop to offset the exquisite hand-woven textiles.

LEFT: This four-poster bed has been draped with crisp, white organdie cotton, which has a simple ladder stitch running through it at intervals. It is a perfect example of how to create privacy while maintaining the view.

TOP RIGHT: Lightweight and cool – nothing competes with the comfort of crisp cotton.

CENTRE RIGHT: Embroidered designs and patterns on cotton and linen offer an unobtrusive textured effect.

BELOW RIGHT: Sheer slip-covers in white make an elegant dressing for occasional chairs.

BELOW: Pale-coloured stitching in this cotton cushion cover, with an olive wicker chair, works for an organic palette. The look is soft and subdued, and completely natural.

RIGHT: A basket-weave, woven cotton has been used to cover this contemporary styled sofa. Ecru and chocolate-coloured raffia cushions are piled invitingly on top.

BELOW: Pamper yourself with textural pleasures that are heaven to touch. Try cashmere or velvet for the epitome of sensual luxury. This Zen-inspired bedroom setting is created with a Japanese futon, Tatami mats and an artful layering of vibrant colours and textures on Yoruba cloth, red chenille cushions and a cherry-coloured throw.

RIGHT: Textural interest in this living room appears boldly in the form of ruby-coloured Egyptian Bedouin rugs and a sofa in burgundy-coloured corduroy.

A wooden day-bed is an interesting and natural alternative to a sofa, which complements the wooden trestle table and floor. This setting reflects a proportioned balance of contemporary and traditional elements.

LEFT: Piles of fringed woollen textiles, waffle-weave hand towels, Hampton linen and blanket-stitched throws make wonderful home accessories. They may be shifted around to suit changing moods, seasons and trends.

Throw fabric over a bed and instantly change the ambience in a room, or add chunky weaves for textural impact. Introduce luxurious wool or linen weaves to sofas, pillows and beds for snuggling up in cooler weather.

RIGHT: Fabric may be stretched over panels or frames and displayed in a way that decoratively fills a vast space. Combinations of natural and artificial materials complement each other in soothing shades of pink and green, inspired by nature. The stark, stainless-steel detail on the chairs is a welcome contrast to the rich, warm hues of the wooden flooring.

LEFT: A perfect nest for lazy summer days has been created with these beautifully woven textiles found in locations all over Africa. Casually placed upon a wooden daybed and grass mat, the silk throw and cushion covers complete a comfortable and relaxed afternoon setting.

ABOVE: A healthy environment in which to live: natural sisal flooring and pure cotton sheets are kind to our bodies and pleasing to the touch.

ABOVE AND RIGHT: A kelim from Afghanistan adds bold visual

contrast to earthy, plastered walls and a sandstone floor. Functional

and beautiful, this piece is displayed to its full splendour when it is

used as a curtain and drawn closed.

LEFT AND RIGHT: Intricate patterns draw the eye, and complex arrangements tempt us to look again, to feel and sometimes to gaze with wonder at the design. Use textiles to highlight a display of personal treasures, or layers of soft fabrics to create spaces that radiate serenity and comfort.

RAW

RAW

FIBRE

Natural fibres such as sisal, coir, sea grass, raffia, jute, hemp and banana leaves are all hardy, easy-to-care-for coverings ideal for a warm climate. They are available in a myriad savanna-tinted hues.

Sisal is a tough, long-lasting fibre traditionally used in Kenya for roofing and making baskets. Sisal and coir share a distinctive coarseness which, when used for floor matting, is therapeutic for bare feet. Jute is a soft, silky fibre – as it is not particularly resilient, it is often mixed with other natural fibres to add strength. Jute can be found in anything from wrapping paper to cloth.

Hessian is also a coarse fabric, usually made from a blend of jute and hemp. A rough and versatile fibre, hemp is now in demand by consumers for its durability and texture. Ideal for floor rugs, throws and unusual window coverings, it creates a rugged, rustic look that celebrates the natural environment.

Other useful and beautiful fibres are the illala palm, bamboo and the grasses grown for thatching and basketry. They can all be sculpted and woven into sofas, chairs and screens. They are naturally water repellent, cool in summer and warm in winter .

These fibres come from renewable resources, making them important in a sustainable environmental system – they are the ultimate eco-friendly option when it comes to surfaces that need to put up with a rigorous lifestyle. Commercial support of traditionally made woven crafts ensures that this ancient skill and knowledge will always remain part of our African and global heritage.

PREVIOUS PAGE: Simple sea-grass matting enhances this informal Zen-style dinner setting.
RIGHT: Casual-fibre floor coverings like this sisal rug add texture, which is offset – in this room –
by the smooth lines of the lavishly upholstered leather sofa.

BELOW: Grass matting, banana leaves, sisal and raffia are excellent natural fabrics for everyday items such as coasters, exfoliating loofahs, bags and lampshades. The natural coarseness of raw-fibre slippers provide a gentle massage.

BELOW: Scour the markets in your home area or holiday destination for favourite ethnic crafts, and use them for storage or display. A collection of hand-woven baskets will add symmetry to a sparsely decorated room.

LEFT: Serene whites and organic sandstone add up to a peaceful bathroom. Grass matting infuses the cool, pale interior with warm, earthy tones. Light, space and raw

materials are like a soothing tonic at the end of an energetic day.

ABOVE: A cinder-block supported table and a hemp rug create a laid-back, nomadic look.

BELOW: The careful selection of clean lines and raw-fibre floor coverings (sisal and coir) in this living area co-ordinates simplicity with luxury.

RIGHT: The bamboo window screen, ladder and side table in this bedroom live in happy fusion with the rich yet soft tones of the wooden headboard (made from a Tonga door). The embroidered throws and silk cushions soften the impact, allowing all the elements to combine comfortably.

BELOW: Use wicker baskets to store or display personal items.

RIGHT: Sisal, shown here, is a tough and lasting fibre from the *Agava sisalana*, a cactus-like plant that grows naturally in tropical climates. Suitable for whole rooms or as matting and runners, it is available in a fine or heavy bouclé in varied designs and colours.

Sisal, coir, jute and hemp are natural choices when decorating with raw wood and hand-plastered walls.

LEFT: Sea grass is another versatile fibre — and it has nothing to do with the sea; in fact, it is cultivated inland.

Sea grass, along with other natural fibres, is finding its way in to every accessory and onto most domestic surfaces. These days, for example, there are sisal-covered ice buckets, woven grass mats, baskets and coasters, raffia handbags and wicker serving trays.

These products celebrate traditional weaving methods, which are a large part of our African and global heritage. And when it comes to aesthetic appeal, they have no competition from their artificial counterparts.

LEFT AND RIGHT: Bamboo, the great towering fibrous grass, is not to be underestimated. Flexible, lightweight and resilient, it has been used for centuries as a building material. Bamboo poles make good fencing as well as false roofing to conceal unsightly ceilings. When bamboo is split it may also be made into garden gates and wall panels and woven into hats, mats or baskets. It is even made into food – in many countries bamboo shoots are an exotic treat. Bamboo propagates easily with a good supply of water, and is often seen growing on steep hillsides to prevent soil erosion.

LEFT AND RIGHT:

Modern design is plain

and minimal. It has been

achieved successfully in

this living area through the choice of contemporary furniture pieces made

from natural materials. The clean lines are offset by the rough textural quality

of the wicker chair and sisal floor covering. Simple and uncluttered, this

interior exudes peace.

LEFT AND RIGHT: Woven baskets and bowls make decorative storage containers – with their different weaves and designs they add strong textural elements to an interior. These traditional grass mats from Japan and North Africa complete simple table settings.

The popularity of natural fibres prevents traditional knowledge from being eroded by the proliferation of artificial alternatives.

SUPPLIERS

SOUTH AFRICA

Wood

Rare Woods
12 Nourse Avenue
Epping Road, Industria,
Cape Town
Tel: (021) 535-2004

Stable Marketing
16 Nyman Street
Kensington, Maitland, Cape
Town
Tel: (021) 593-5540

Suntups Wooden Flooring
111 Hartzenbergfontein
Walkerville, Johannesburg
Tel: (011) 949-1009

Rustic Wood Furniture
Tel: (011) 791-0976

T & B Log Homes
Vigilante Drive
Industrial Area, Knysna
Tel: (044) 382 5442

Marble, stone, ceramic and mosaic

Fine Art Marble
37 Paarden Eiland Road
Paarden Eiland, Cape Town
Tel: (021) 510-8333

Marble Classic
6 Loper Avenue
Spartan, Johannesburg
Tel: (011) 392-6700

Mazista Tiles
233 Hans Strijdom Drive
Northriding, Johannesburg
Tel: (011) 462-4440

Natural Tile Products
99 Gabriel Road
Plumstead, Cape Town
Tel: (021) 761-1175

Mosaic Arts
107 Siersteen Street
Silvertondale, Pretoria
Tel: (012) 804-7392

Just Tiles
25 Hunter Street
Durban
Tel: (031) 332-8581

Fibre: sisal, coir and jute

Kashgar
Shop 136, The Mall
Rosebank
Tel: (011) 442-9092

Rebtex
11 Purlin Road
Isando, Johannesburg
Tel: (011) 974-8951

Albert Carpets
Roland Square
66 Roland Street,
Cape Town
Tel: (021) 462-3446

Rowley & Hughes
Central Park
Unit 4, Hopkins Street
Salt River, Cape Town
Tel: (021) 447-0075

Carpet Creations
320 Stamford Hill Road
Durban
Tel: (031) 303-2750

Metal, wrought iron and pewter

Moroccan Warehouse
Avalon Building
Cnr. Hope & Mill Streets
Gardens, Cape Town
Tel: 083 261 8061

Creative Spaces
71 Loop Street,
Cape Town
Tel: (021) 423-9772

Metalu
PO Box 750
28 Nicholson Road,
Denver, Bedfordview,
Johannesburg
Tel: (011) 616-5392

Textiles and fabrics

The Linen Gallery
434 Old Pretoria Road,
Midrand, Johannesburg
Tel: (011) 315-5482

St Leger & Viney
28A Kildare Road
Newlands, Cape Town
Tel: (021) 683-5233/4

Mavromac
5 Wolfe Street
Wynberg, Cape Town
Tel: (021) 797-4739/
(031) 303-8203

Home Fabrics
60 Old Pretoria Road
Halfway House, Midrand
Johannesburg
Tel: (011) 266-3800

Timbuktu Trading
Unit1, Progress Park
48 Richards Drive, Midrand
Johannesburg
Tel: (011) 315-2363/08

Cecile & Boyd's
253 Florida Road
Morningside, Durban
Tel: (031) 312-3589

Plaster, cement and concrete

Cretestone Plaster Finishes
Johannesburg
Tel: (011) 788-6939
or Cape Town
Tel: 083 289-6638

BPB Gypsum
Garret Street
Parrow Industries,
Cape Town
Tel: (021) 959-5019
or
3 Van Lingen Street
Industrial East, Johannesburg
Tel: (011) 825-3622

Cemcrete
8 Telford Street
Industria, Johannesburg
Tel: (011) 474-2415

Cement & Concrete
Institute
Portland Park
Pretoria Main Road,
Halfway House
Tel: (011) 315-0300

UNITED KINGDOM

Wood

The Real Wood Furniture
Company
60 Oxford Street
Woodstock, Oxfordshire
Tel: (01993) 81-3887

Stone, ceramic, mosaic and glass tiles

Mosaics Direct
Freephone (0800) 035-3232
www.mosaics.co.uk

Reed Harris
Riverside House
27 Carnwath Road, Fulham
London, SW6 3HR
Tel: (020) 7736-7511

Stone Age Ltd
19 Filmer Road
London, SW6 7BU
Tel: (020) 7385-7954
(80 types of stone, plus
slate, all cut to size)

Fibre: sisal, coir, jute and seagrass

Fired Earth
117-119 Fulham Road
London, SW3 6RL
Tel: (020) 7589-0489

Natural Flooring Direct
46 Webbs Road
London, SW11 6SF
Tel: (020) 7228-2042
(also bamboo)

Metal floor and wall tiles

Metalkitsch
50 Bath Street
The Maltings, Gravesend
Kent, DL6 3SG
Tel: (01474) 56-8229
Fax: (01474) 35-1110
www.metalkitsch.co.uk

Aluminium, steel, zinc and stainless steel

London Metal Centre
Tel: (020) 8694-6022
Fax: (020) 8694-6249
Email:
londonmetal@yahoo.com
(Call for European and
national stockists)

Wrought iron

The Iron Design Company
Summer Carr Farm
Thornton Le Moor
Northallerton
North Yorkshire
Mail Order Tel: (01609)
77-8143

Architectural Ironmongery

Arnold & Oakley
28 Kyrie Street
Ross-on-Wye
Herefordshire, HR9 7DB
Tel/Fax: (01989) 56-7946
(Mail Order available)

Textiles and fabrics

Osborne & Little
304-308 King's Road
London, SW3 5UH
Tel: (020) 7352-1456

Fabrics Direct
Tel: (0800) 975-7296
Fax: (0800) 975-7297
www.fabricdirect.co.uk

Plaster, cement and concrete

B & Q
Head Office
Portswood House
1 Hampshire Corporate
Park, Chandlers Ford
Eastley, Hants, SO53 3YX
Tel: (0800) 11-1810
(Call for details of your
nearest store)

Focus Do-It-All Group Ltd
Head Office
Gawsworth House
Westmere Drive
Crewe, Cheshire
Tel: (0800) 43-6436
(Call for details of your
nearest store)

NEW ZEALAND

Wood

South Pacific Timbers
Cnr Ruru & Shaddock Sts,
Auckland City
Tel: (09) 378-6457
or
7 Bowden Road
Mt Wellington, Auckland
Tel: (09) 573-1144

Rosenfeld Kidson
513 Mt Wellington Highway
Mt Wellington, Auckland
Tel: (09) 573-0503
Fax (09) 573-0504

NZ Hardwood Limited
23 Patiki Road
Avondale, Auckland
Tel: (09) 828-5449
Fax: (09) 820-2460

Kauri Warehouse
28 Saleyards Road
Otahuhu, Auckland
Tel: (09) 276-7633

Country Road Homeware
Freephone (0800) 10-5655
157 Broadway
Newmarket, Auckland
Tel: (09) 524-9685

or
Lambton Quay, Wellington
Tel: (04) 473-1871
or
120 Cashel Street
Christchurch
Tel: (03) 366-7870

furnish.co.nz
Tel: (03) 442-8867
Fax (03) 442-8897
www.furnish.co.nz

Marble, stone, ceramic and mosaic

Trethewey Granite & Marble
Wellington
Tel: (04) 567-5198
or
Auckland
Tel: (09) 827-3017
or
Christchurch
Tel: (03) 348-0680

Stone Craft Enterprises
189-191 Marua Road
Ellerslie, Auckland
Tel: (09) 526-4580
Fax (09) 579-0583
Email:
sales@stonecraft.co.nz

Tile Warehouse
Branches nationwide
Freephone (0800) 28-9845

Jacobsen Creative Surfaces
Freephone (0800) 80-0460
228 Orakei Road
Remuera, Auckland
Tel: (09) 524-1460
Fax (09) 523-1047
or
96 Hutt Street
Kaiwharawhara, Wellington

Tel: (04) 472-8528
Fax (04) 472-8530
or
314 Manchester Street
Christchurch
Tel: (03) 366-4153
Fax (03) 366-6660

Brasell & Ojala Spatial
Concepts
92 Franklin Road
Freemans Bay, Auckland
Tel: (09) 360-3375

Designa Ceramic Tiles
15 Kaimia Street
Ellerslie, Auckland
Tel: (09) 579-0714
or
35 Mandeville Street
Riccarton, Christchurch
Tel: (03) 348-1099
or
128 Gorge Road
Queenstown
Tel: (03) 442-4999

Fibre: sisal, coir and jute

Advance Flooring Company
PO Box 13184, Auckland
Freephone (0508) 23-8262
or Tel: (09) 634-3691

Bespoke Mat Company
162 Jervois Road, Herne
Bay, Auckland
Tel: (09) 360-6044
fax (09) 360-6045
www.bespoke.co.nz

Cane Factory and
Upholstery Shop
39 Lake Road, Hamilton
Tel: (07) 847-2246

Woodnotes' range
(available from Matisse)
125 The Strand
Parnell, Auckland
Tel: (09) 302-2284
or
23 Allen Street, Wellington
Tel: (04) 801-2121

Bamboo Specialists
833 West Coast Road
Oratia, Auckland
Tel: (09) 814-9847

Wicker Imports Ltd
6 Ward Street
New Lynn, Auckland
Tel: (09) 827-6101
Fax (09) 827-6102

Metal, wrought iron and pewter

Iron Worx Engineering
Tel: (025) 90-9642

MetalWerks
30 Gaunt Street
Freemans Bay, Auckland
Tel: (09) 358-2044

Mercer Stainless Ltd
PO Box 71099, Rosebank,
Auckland
Tel: (09) 820-6165
Fax (09) 820-7019

Chapman Engineering Ltd
15 Klondyke Drive
Hornby, Christchurch
Tel: (03) 349-0200
Fax (03) 349-0203

Steelfort
Palmerston North
Tel: (06) 350-1350
Freefax (0508) 78-3353
www.steelfort.co.nz

Textiles and fabrics

Swinson Wallcoverings
104 Carlton Gore Road
Newmarket, Auckland
Freephone (0800) 47-9467
Fax (09) 520-3390
or
19 Tory Street, Wellington
Tel: (04) 385-7574
Fax (04) 384-5091

Designsource
1/7 Axis Building
1 Cleveland Road
Parnell, Auckland
Tel: (09) 309-8816

Cavalier Bremworth
Stockists Nationwide
Freephone (0800) 22-8254
www.cavbrem.co.nz

'Woolscape' from Wools
of New Zealand
Stockists Nationwide
Freephone (0800) 49-6657
www.woolsnz.com

Plaster, cement and concrete

Peter Fell Ltd
81-83 Patiki Road
Avondale, Auckland
Freephone (0800) 42-2656
Tel: (09) 828-6460
Fax (09) 820-0722

Firth Industries
Branches Nationwide
Freephone (0800) 80-0576

Placemakers
Branches Nationwide
Freephone (0800) 425-2269